Landscapes I & II

Also by Lesle Lewis

Small Boat

Landscapes

I & II

Lesle Lewis

Alice James Books
FARMINGTON, MAINE

ACKNOWLEDGEMENTS

I am grateful to the editors of the following magazines in whose pages some of these poems first appeared, sometimes in earlier versions: *American Letters & Commentary*, *Barrow Street*, *Pool*, *Old Crow*, *Mudfish*, *Massachusetts Review*, *New Hampshire Review*, *Double Room* and *Sentence*.

10 9 8 7 6 5 4 3 2 1

Alice James Books are published by Alice James Poetry Cooperative, Inc., an affiliate of the University of Maine at Farmington.

ALICE JAMES BOOKS
238 MAIN STREET
FARMINGTON, ME 04938

www.alicejamesbooks.org

Library of Congress Cataloging-in-Publication Data
Lewis, Lesle.
Landscapes I & II / Lesle Lewis
    p.   cm.
ISBN-13: 978–1–882295–54–8 (pbk.)
ISBN-10: 1–882295–54–4 (pbk.)
1. Prose poems, American. I. Title.
PS3612.E967L36 2006
811'.54—dc22   2005029146

Alice James Book gratefully acknowledges support from the University of Maine at Farmington and the National Endowment for the Arts. ❦

Cover Art: Rick Klauber, "Strut," 2003.

For Pops

CONTENTS

Landscapes I & II

Story

You, my girl, I don't dislike. Faith is a male. This is a love story. Doubt is a character too and her sidekick, self appraisal. Patience is another character if you hang around him enough. Death plays itself. If the boy is an innocent, he believes the girl will be the only one. She knows love is temporary but she loves the boy. Along comes the poet who sits on a bench, watches, and cries. It is so beautiful and more than that. So is everything against the poor boy? Along comes a man. He's willing to wait and see. He feels no stress either way. Maybe he wants it to work for the boy; he probably does. Who doesn't love the little man? In the end, death itself shows and clicks the characters off one by one. What's left? The love lingers in the air. The doubt hovers. The patience stays patient. Nothing is lost. Spring comes to all of us.

Research for Happiness

I fell and banged my head hard on the floor, then banged it again with intention.

There was "brilliant summer scenery."

My hand danced out the window.

Water drops made mandalas, fruit tarts, faces.

I could see Arthur and Camilla's house, the chicken house, a rabbit, a plot of house plants, and behind it all, the voluptuous ocean.

Later, I would walk through the grounds to the loveliest of pools where the moon was shimmering.

Who swims in the pool?

Small winds and a flock of sisters.

Change in the Grove of Chickadees

Happy for nothing, we could be with no dinner to cook.

Absence is gigantic in our heads and houses.

We're old and it's bold to say so standing at the kitchen counter with the flashing red things.

The clock says midnight and we say yes.

When we go out, time always pays.

We spike our heads with copper ions and picnic with the breast explorers.

We're riding the earth.

Non-motion is impossible.

At Wellman Pond

In one of many cities of the many coming springtimes, one man becomes two. You keep your soul in your dog.

One thought lies on top of another on top of another. They don't keep each other warm but flatten each other, and finally they are quiet. I am the quietest one. My flatness lies here. His head peers over the table.

The room is shaped like this: this, the odd chance that we are happening. In residence kitty curls the end of time absolute too. It dawns like dawn I'm looking at my own, something to put here I'm just dying to write. It was April the spoon-bender's daughter caught her miracle. She's happy and I'm judgmental. This time it will end differently.

Call it a city; into the ruined city in the vaulted chambers of your heart we'll go. From the rubble, from the underbelly of it, in the sweet yards, light shafts shift.

There's equal distance ahead, equal behind, and equal distance to flow from the social kitchen. She's upped her meds. He's made a pork roast stuffed with prunes and apricots. Another she is waiting, all charm and loveliness. She looks at water flowing through an ice maple leaf and there finds saintly poses and all of the handmaidens' bathing places.

Imagine the working and the really working, the heart when it's not working. Will they name a waterfall for you? No, but you'll get to sleep in a funny little town where the townspeople and swine have drawn together. Inside their mazy brains, I've got a cot for napping through the afternoons in a moment amongst my forebears.

Whatever it is and is called, hypomania, spring, I won't get up until it's forty degrees to be friendly by the fire. Winter was a monster. Do we need our winters to see how spring is meant?

From the Cave of Questions

Abstraction puts on her cowboy boots. Who else would walk the boundaries with you and photograph your pears?

The trees drip psychedelia. The sky is stormy. The model is boney. When a question of intelligence emerges into daylight, she squints. How dumb am I? Narcotics and light feed her. Folding laundry, she removes herself. Where have I already been this morning? The sun splashes on the bed, the mother drowns her children, a man is upset and has a gun. The world has urgencies. In fact, you're out of it. It comes as you lie by the running dam. "Who are you?" It says my reason, my antidepressant.

When I get back from New York, France becomes serious. Where I stand is the blue behind clouds. For the sake of an argument, let's say you put your feet up and decide to write. There are no flowers around. "The key is in the bars in the *s* in the *w.*"

Baudelaire's Mouth

The past is a gas, a vapor, an odor really only, from which "the simple division, by the lips."

Who wants to go back to that terrible time?

You were only that little bride, perfect novella length.

The picture of the world dropped off the wall.

A big force told you you're special.

That little king is seventy-seven years away, a man with a tail.

There's no way to easily live then, but your life is easy.

"I do portraits."

Your compromise is to do everything.

I am also a very busy cartoon.

My head spirals, stars, moons, and birds.

New Snow Cover

Home is a mess. She's lost in theory land. Her head's in a bag. She spits on herself and rips her pants. She makes everyone listen to silence and has no money for the tip.

New snow cover.

Now we might be the ones who will be so successful and quote ourselves. Our November bodies affirm our quest driven by an acceptance of our dissatisfaction that fuels it, the meat of our sandwiches.

Something Else Coincides

You live on a big farm in heaven. You sit on a blanket and watch fun people sing show tunes.

The crack in the ice is the train track going back to New York. It's exactly the same thing. You say the only thing: "Thank you."

You can save yourself for tomorrow or you can spend yourself every day. You can beat up the poets before they all go bleak.

A Giant Orange

I look a wreck. I look myself.

The tiniest of marks marks the horizon drawing us. Otherwise it's no landscape. If you get even a glimpse of the great complexity, you might as well die. A hot wave of nothing swims by.

The water will stay in the pond. Someone else would live here if we didn't. The fish snap at flies. If we had more money . . . .

A boat of a leaf on the surface of the mind with the others of its kind floats.

You are chasing an escaped horse, crossing a roaring brook, and boom! Morning stands there. Like the dog with a stick he'll do anything for, between the parrot feathers in the water pot, the lily blooms a giant orange. My name is Pokey with an *e*.

The Mother of Day

Like cold rains make things green, we are fortunates with depressive tendencies. Hear the steam machine?

We smooth the seconds' heads of hair as they streak by. Occasionally we hold and rock the miniature or monster minutes.

We trust the voices that appear out of ice cube trays. They start cold and warm up as they speak and gesture. They are only about themselves.

The mother of day calls, "Come, come."

One way to build a bridge is to walk on it. The faith of the nesting goose gives us the faith. We ride the open paper boats.

Five Little Landscapes

The Leaf

The summer community left you a leaf punched with a thousand tiny holes.

Then at the Symposium for Art and Entertainment, the doctors burrowed in and removed the leaf from you and its reflection which had been floating in a valentine-shaped pool.

Stump with Birdwing Shape

The pageant's gone by. The resplendent view instructed and "henceforth I shall be hard to please." That is you taught me how to love, that is, not completely.

Correction

Troops of friends and helpers of winter unite in the mountains and with their hands out confess.

Not all conversations meet in the middle, so the artist's vision frequently corrects the writer's sympathy.

Dear Future

I can't be the queen. I am the cranky baby just like a waxy bird, and I don't build myself up.

Lap is not a technical term, only a place when you sit you can offer to my deficiencies. You could not be conscious of the large and small infinities. Every view has its description, every room its acoustics, each its antics, dear future.

I was on the train talking to you on my cell. My teachers and I were dancing. My sister was so happy and my husband was playing the piano.

A Bunch of Harpies

The horizon divides me from the coincidences of temptation and desire which are no coincidence but distant and moving away with purpose in the stream whose purpose we don't know which leaves us shaking with awe. At the same time cold beauties descend from the hills we see. They want us to recognize them.

Small Being

We take our small beating organs to seating positions on the floor.

So we can begin to touch the beginning of knowing what to do, a small being begins ignored by the larger people.

Let's not rush it.

Her innocence is useful and more than that, it's a pleasure.

She puts pennies on our toes and our knees because we need things of value given to us.

Her expression is the best that can be and she hopes to steer us to goodness.

What's not good is not this.

Success Doesn't Matter

Flowers explode in our faces and then petals rain down, the best we've ever seen.

We are celebrating live chickens and ducks.

We see seal heads popping up all around the salvages.

We have a Mark adventure unsuccessfully; success doesn't matter.

We are gassing up the boat or holding down the porch.

We start off with everything we don't know and then children come along on the rocks and don't see us.

Blue Hackensack

It's your tea to my coffee, my journal to yours. Sitting up is good for your lungs.

We fix time to keep the clock. We move to a general ward because you are better, but the general ward makes me sick.

In my absence, your feet hold down my newspaper, my community, and my intelligence. Finally my nightcap. Finally you take the injection. Finally a picture of death I understand. It's only one terrible inch long.

Mint greens throb and wave. Train ticket-punched stars fall down in waves. Your first name becomes, became, your last. The town's run over by the blue vapors of its residents.

Flight of the Zeppelin

Where did my boots go? Do I only imagine I had boots? Where is Balzac going with Swedenborg?

I'll study harder. I'll build a larger brain cottage of rain planks by the woodland pool with those circles that ripple my reflected world. Surprising myself, from the bank, I'll dive into it.

It's a long trip. And deep, the water is sky.

The Smaller Vegetarians

You do not interrupt, so you listen to lots of nonsense. Some of it grows on you and you become moss-covered. Your existence totters.

The story of your morning walk is a dread. One thing leads to the next and it still does. You feel some afternoonishness. Your cat sleeps on a hard dance floor until she hears the smaller vegetarians foraging.

I feel your breathing and that you've turned towards me.

Without You

You are the good citizen and not the poet.

You want explanations beautiful, but not the truth which calls for more compassion than you can muster.

You've had some accidents and some illnesses and some lovers.

Can we talk?

Your love life might interest me, your childhood, your current health issues.

For me, it's always you, you, you.

It's No Small Thing to Be Yourself

I thought (think) perhaps not.

We flew to the music and painting land, a land more wise than benevolent, with more water than mountain.

In the nonphysical photograph, you and I linked necks.

Oh holy bunny! Oh pearl bracelet!

Oh, this is being too high!

This is the other half of our property.

Shooting the Bear

Like the novel in verse, the novel in verse, dogs in this town drive cars.

Houses expose themselves slowly.

It's flammable linseed oil to which the cabinetmaker who made our feeders after losing his fingers loses his shop.

We must think of the little nun's happiness.

If we shoot the bear, it won't bother the feeders.

The birds love our willow trees, and love *is* the word.

Lover with Flowers

We give this difficult time of year for its youth and stupidity the keys to the car.

Art books flip themselves open.

Weeks tick past the hanging moon. Crocuses close at night.

Small yards boast exquisite water gardens.

A ship lands and from it debark the sailors of it, unaccustomed to land.

I am unaccustomed.

Shopping

Drops accumulate in one spot on the windowsill. We waste light and intelligence. The snow softens and we can sled. We give cardamom seeds to Sheila. Mark moves our old piano to Susan's. The voice of a flowerpot speaks.

Ghosts travel through foreign cities of narrow streets, a gathering of strangers unto shopping, unto sickness, unto death, the accumulation of ornaments, of nothing, of robes and furs.

Night dies at light in the trees' pink moment. How clean the rhododendron leaves! Our chairs yawn.

Change of Plans

The Sunoco clock flashes: boom, girls, go.

Hear the rain crash, hard to hear with windows open.

We carry our fragments in small purses. Only fifty dollars?

We were high in the woods of Tyringham. We came to True North.
It was like a boat, our bed. He called me Venus.

I allow myself two small lines, to read Gertrude to the cats, to be
your pet poet.

I mean you're not a state-of-the-world barometer.

I could go to New Jersey as late as Wednesday and stay until
Sunday.

Vivia, Mistress of the Small Landscape

Mistress of the Small Landscape, I forget your name.

Most Serene Republic of the Interior, I need your advice.

Can we practice affection, ma'am?

If you cannot surrender yourself enough, my birdy friend, that's what drugs are for.

Dear Vivia, you linger in liquidity.

I Love Lenora

Under a cloud over New Haven, our train is unmoving.

We were born once; we walked through forests; we tried to save ourselves and our belongings; our fathers died and went away in boats.

We are drifters, I tried to tell you, handsome.

The Moth and the Time

Friends and relatives run through the century. You choose this wall for how it might be rain falling into itself. Kids run through the paper room. Who pinks the light? It's been a long while since you've said "hi." You feel kind of glorious. You are a four-legged table as much as anything. Read about yourself; your ex-girlfriend is your dead possum of springtime.

Let it be ragged, your life hung out on a line. You have to invent some pretty big rules not to break them. I'll direct myself to you. Why can't I let you love anyone you'd like? I can't be two people and only two.

Invention turns a person on his head, shrinks him to a cherub, or turns him into a girl and her mom and a giant push thing. "What happened?" "I don't know. What happened?" "You were dreaming." Will contemplation flower into knowing? Did you do your one exceptionally good deed today?

The barn falls down on the boat in it. A man trains his pig to jump. The royal family farm grows; the king grows rotund and the culture advances. A vague boulder hovers in the sky sometimes.

Meanwhile, I've hung a clock for you in the garden. It gongs nine times to say ten. I kiss you goodnight and you kiss me goodbye. The left train track becomes conscious of the right, kind of an archway tunnel of coming and going.

In the regular order of life, I forgive misdeeds. My perseverance leads to my humiliation. The call is on the ground and it will be no barnyard. I have no idea what time it is or who is in the house.

Kava Time

To relax our positions and to lie flat naked on the grass, we've found pause.

The scent of rosemary consumes us.

Think of me as pasted to your back and looking backwards which is my forwards; if you're lying on your stomach, I'm looking at the sky.

It's all an even whirr of moths and Tao and pills.

A Theory of Sustenance

We drove by, dropping meds in the depressed storm drains. The horizon was depicted to pretend it's some distance, not flat infinity in your face.

If you loved some non-person, if it were simple, you'd know it. You'd stand corrected and sober. If you wore black and white and thought your experience worth reading about, you'd be wrong on both counts.

I am an expert. Not that I can copy anything great, but I have learned to fathom as if it were a very pure form of long-necked loving.

Wouldn't it be wise to be sharp and weigh our lives in this moment before extreme life bursts loose on the wetlands?

Experiment

I can think of my world as sixteen squares with a mountain, a house roof, a church steeple, trees of reds and greens, and a sky, to place within.

It's raining.

I can move my head all around.

The light changes frequently.

A fly creeps along the window glass.

I can think of my head as sixteen squares.

I can move the world all around.

A fly creeps along the window glass.

Bumblebee Love

I have no idea what I'm looking at. Is it an alligator with a smaller alligator in its mouth? The musicians smile at me. I am a woman sideways. I am leaning into you.

You drive along the farms that edge the lake until you get to the end of the world for a cup of coffee. You have a guitar and a shawl because that's how I see you as both subject and poetry evolving. You meet yourself in passing, you fallen journalist, you duckling, you tower of power over me. I've bought you lots of man things.

11:53 Milwaukee time. The museum is quiet. You are the wooden floor. You are the lake too large to go around. You are the snake family. You live under the world tree with your intellectuals. You are a prostitute and my friend. You have ninety-nine names. You are the land. I'd like to say finally who you are. I'm interested in your animals.

You say that many people in your village have been killed. Is your pain constant or throbbing? I will make myself your friend over a long time. Who else would lie down with the bumblebees?

You are not my love, but love. After love, the grasses sway like almost loving. We shouldn't call it loving.

The days grow shorter very slowly. We talk about suicide, and do we really think New Hampshire is separate from Vermont? How the ferns let the path and the path lets the ferns! These are the days we dream of and the wind blows them for us. The brook travels into the pond in a necklace of continuous and's. Summer travels like an ant over the bricks in a cricket-laced light. We're not having drinks anymore.

Awaiting Your Reply

Lapsang souchang runs through me like a train through daffodils, construction delays, and a truckload of feisty animals. I'm going under to it. We're all interested in how the toy pump-up plane flies in great circles, then crashes somewhere new each time. And we're forced to think about the holes in the ground as lack of ground, although we know lacks are things too.

I disturbed some wildlife. The heron screamed and the turtle flailed and the geese yelled at me violently. When I paddled away, I gave them some minutes of relief and joy.

Now the air's made misty by trees' bud babies in long stretches of minutes. I'm getting happier now and my headache is gone, what might have been a huge pumpkin rock or an urn for hoses. Deep rest happens in the wilderness.

Does beyond self have to include the others? They want summer notes and light to last a winter, the superior sleeping behavior of warm-blooded dreamers, to sit on their haunches in the light and be what's called being. Standing on rounded corners hurts their backs.

Wrapping Paper

There was a singing by the river, and no one but me was thinking of me. It was the last class and we had to read a dense page that said everything. We were pushed. We bicycled away. Joy did not climb or fall.

Finally I'm falling behind. Finally I'm not the first. I've never been. You've been a fierce thinker who scares people to death. I am doing a lot of meditation. Or you could say, the relationships all snap and everyone is lonely.

Yours Is a Contemplative Wine

The sun is setting from her terrace the color of tomatoes. Inside her clothes is her body and inside her body is another body that is a smile not shaped like a smile but shaped exactly like the inside of her body so happy to be with you.

Like dripping water nonstop from the fountain, your golden light is coming all over the place. All over the place is this: her not knowing anything but you.

Her skinned animal life hangs over your sink. When the clock strikes eight sobs for your parting, it's no longer nameless what she longs for. Sometimes it's a boat; sometimes she's a dragonfly. Sometimes you're a suntan lotion traveler, sometimes plums.

The Wart Hog As an Example

Poor Jeff's girl's gone to Wyoming with a sports car, lipstick, and a rock to dance on. Jeff carries a board. Jeff carries in a box of nails. My name in my head wakes me. I've slept stupidly. Does Cynthia want to marry Ryan? Does Sarah want to marry Adam? Does Adam want to marry Sarah? Remember tea in Tambacounda? Jeff is done unloading the truck. Your need makes me guilty but I'm not going to your party.

The electrician knows the man who said hi who is the man who runs the sandwich shop. What American music do they play? Greatness could leak out, white tablecloths shine. I've got the best table. I thought the word was "beautiful." People are themselves. Napkins come out.

When you killed a chicken, it was clean, when he killed a goat, she thought it was a wild bird. We'll drink tea until the cows come home and newspapers stop printing and we can have a pot to pee in. We have a beautiful new wellness center. We are selling cattle, one for the village.

We need our mail. They don't have any. It's absurd to live without absurdity. We see also through our ears sometimes all the nothingness. I try to think about it all. Helicopter accidents and dragonflies, in the same world, hostages and group love, a turtle, a wart hog, twenty-two thousand miles. Excellent, but I could do more.

Oh, to Be a Non-Complainer!

You see into the mirror and into the mirror. You're tired of looking into the mush, but you don't want to turn off the stereo. Your eyes suck your face into your brain.

What a great face! What a new person! You dreamed about this, but you thought it was a dream about friends.

You look forth. You find the death of books, of time, of cool, of all the people. You feel like a bunch of desperate coins that can't be spent in America.

Look out from yourself. You're not sleeping at night thinking. The work must get harder. It will feel like this particle of blackness.

The four seasons will fall, recover, rise, and leap.

You'll be happy for the first time in days, only days.

Glad for Things Pretty to Think

Old ladies go out of the café one door and come back in the other.
You see, they had lunch but forgot to look at the chocolates.

Our backs ache and the world presents beauty. War in the world
aches and the world presents beauty.

Good Mood and Bad Mood sit quietly next to each other in
matching rocking chairs.

A three-inch person emerges from the far side of the lawn, and its
bigger-than-the-person voice commands us.

A Pipe, a Teacher, a Train

We have to drift someplace to stop thinking one thought and then another.

So, if tools began civilization, then the way wet bales burn down a barn, thunder is a new thought turning into hard rain which burns down a forest.

Noisy Bird

I saw them hugging in the garden. There's a disconnect. Thus the day began dear dear doctor.

The junk man knew what he wanted for the table they wanted.

They carried soccer balls in their mouths so joyfully.

They will find hats for the wedding and there will hardly be a day gone by.

New Hampshire swirls; they do it all rushed; they're like rushes in the swamps.

They are northern people all banged up.

They are tall as the tall splendid weeds.

They throw kisses to strangers because in their minds the occasion calls for throwing.

I'm good, still good, very okay. My head is a noisy bird with short hair.

Rockabye me in the hammock being so smart and all.

I Hate to Stop Skating

1

Through ice-crusted woods to the beaver pond to skate on a half-sunny cold morning, I hike.

Mother's unwell position in bed is a hill to look about from.

On the fears of loving, no one is my boss.

Cowboy Sam books I can read myself.

"The folds of the swineherd's mantle and his gesture are Greek."

2

I hear the beaver sniffling in their lodge.

Mother's illness is like a perfume bottle.

The book escapes the library and makes a way of thinking utterly tolerant of itself.

"He tells the little horse the whole story."

3

I hate to stop gliding this way, but my feet are cold.

My mother's illness is like the George Washington Bridge.

Oh Amtrak!

Train of questions, oh train! I'm deep into darkness wondering.
Each landscape is a car. Each car is a landscape I go through like a
thought in a brain.

I am having a drink on the train ride to heaven: wet yellow woods,
pumpkin fields, house, house, house, house.

Who is the woman I see from the train sitting in her apartment in
setting sunlight?

Am I the I that gives on the train stopped in Palmer, Massachusetts?

Today's Report

We went to a red-dressed recital on the night of the lunar eclipse. We could be extremely poor in moments of surrender in the maskless happiness of the music. We'd both married humans.

We are rolling, getting good at unknowing, but using a wheelbarrow. Of the twelve ways to move stone, your head from the bed is the first.

Your thoughts are very faithful. Obviously you hiked down the road and up the field and counted the cows in order to make the report: that the world stands some days sideways and trees float off.

Body and Art

Her not small body was too small for the fireball of garbage-growth in her chest glowing and burning orange like a dump fire with a scalloped edge. She was a house with its lights on late. She was on dream house fire. She was the firesetter and called it another sleep that lasted not long enough. In the morning, she wondered what bed with coffee looked like, whether the house was quiet or not, one morning version versus the other with the door closed. Her tenant moved out one box at a time down the icy steps and then black garbage bag by garbage bag.

Human Decency

Sleeping is just giving up. We lose the tree markers; we lose our way which might be the way. We daydream away. We come back after only one day of being dead. We are not the world. We are in the world. We need to reach out to know that there is the world. Who shoots to ruin the peace?

You've left a piece of paper on the table that says, "Money." I've lost that piece of paper. It's still ruining more than it should. You think of me and me of you thinking of me of you, that I see that you see me crying. I am delicate. I see myself and walk away.

My body is not comfortable; it's rural, knock on wood, no big worries but the election. I go by truck, red gloves and pop radio on. Dog's in the bed and gold leaves blow. Small mosses grow in my studio at home. Their veins contribute.

It takes a hundred days to find the angles of the earth that fit our backs. By then we might be sheep. We're on two maps. We are moral philosophy and a new human decency. If you have friends, I hope you can enjoy them.

New Views

Romantic adventures, free of habit yet with reasons, approach on the air.

We're carrying some guilt, or else the chipmunk should eat the cat.

Along come some magic bandaids.

Moss grows on some rusted mushrooms.

The view does not consider us.

How quickly new views become us!

The Gardener's Service Is Complete

On Saint-Gaudens' lawn, the gardener blossoms out another
layer of petals, right where someone might see her. Below her head,
her body disintegrates into concentric doodlings: herbs, boxes,
bottles, urns, wattle fences, central wellheads. The swell spitfire
scent of a beautiful girl, her flower half fool's cap, sparkles under
her feet, a ying yang blossom she won't poo-poo as merely a dream.
Nor will the bronze angel flowering over her a moment now and
now it's almost gone. The sound falling from the angel's lips is solar
dust and settles into her apron pockets. The dusty voice says with
accurate authoritative prophecy that deformity rethought is new
form and so the gardener walks away on her proper proven double
stems.

The Floating Dots, a Waving Sigh

You called twice sad today. Ah, it is as it is.

Sun on ice on beaver pond under power lines skims unwavering
towards who wants to lie on it, who kneels to it.

The way it teases you goodbye, you know it can kill you. You look
beautiful too when beauty showshoes away.

Rabbit Moon

We're hanging on the phone waiting for a change.

Well, it's not good or some good news.

We have one head above the water and one below.

We want our breasts included.

We have coffee thank god and coffee and siblings.

We are embarrassed if we are praised.

The fog is a morning pink; the distance away is spring.

We think this is the path; then we've got the Sally Ann lights off.

* * *

We are black-cloaked bearded figurines for sale, irreconcilable fragments filled with electricity zooming in our offices. Our latches don't fit our other sides. We don't know our own anatomies. We can hardly be objective. We won't have another minute to try.

Not by Name

You are right about the general and the specific, but you thought
I meant tomorrow; I meant last year. You thought I meant you; I
meant the creamy yellow moon, and everyone else. A white craft
drifts downriver between your head and the chimney.

Flying

It really feels terrific to see all this from the sky: the hidden indulgences, the suits for little sirs, the bobby pins on your end table belonging to your girlfriend. Five falling stars follow us and five people who do not see them, and death, an arm reaching out from within a house to close the shutters.

We can undulate just a little and get more momentum. When we get higher, it's all just lines that swirl and a red dot. It's not so much what our hearts are doing.

We find a red car in the snow gone off the road into a tree and a woman is slumped and Portuguese love songs play on her radio.

Non-sentences are how we feel. We're like ice. We're running on it and falling down. We suddenly land and wake from nonexistence. We don't know how to use our hands. It's a private showing of a Warhol film.

Dusk

She comes in minute increments in the temple forest.

Her story's a mess, her plight misted.

Her forced apple blossom forms flit with crying trumpets.

She finds nothing but a cabin sheltering Dostoyevsky and me.

Leaning into her is at least specific.

That's all it takes for her to speak through me to me.

A Dance in the Continuum

You're over-pinked, supper-side up, and earth-side down. Officers circle the swamplands.

You're becoming one of them, zero degrees, all idea, no thing. In fact, the speed of light does not vary because light is always where it's going. Its wrists are curved.

You know by experience the mountains in the mountainous continuum where each of many people live in some form of violet light.

The Rain Hints of Spring

The globular soul falls down like falling downstairs and sits low
at the bottom of guesswork, that jiggle mouse who lying, smiling,
and killing kicks the globate out of bed and out the door where
happenstance finds her a domesticated woodlot and a cow field from
which even at a distance the cows recognize the glob as two-legged.

Brown Bull

If we can determine either position or momentum, the implications are boggling. We can choose either the tendency to exist or to happen. But with a wider receptor theory, it's the end of Either/Or. How long do eggs last in the refrigerator?

We'll never know the full heights and depths of ourselves or the barnyard where tendencies lie, until we find the surprise, the bull, and know to avoid him. I look around for help, but you and your friends are busy dropping trees on the power lines.

Squeaky

I drank hemlock and the taste was not bad. I am not yet feeling effects so I will run around doing a few more things.

The bird hangs from a tree and you can pluck her down, put her beak in your mouth and blow it like a whistle. Death sits anyway like a bird on your shoulder just as was said by my dental hygienist. What's new? What can I do? Look at the sun out there! No one responds.

"I write poetry mostly" seems sad.

We roll our roses with us and a huge red amaryllis. We'll stop to talk to no one. "So how is your flower today?" We don't answer. "Oh my, she's pretty." We don't recognize compliments.

I drink the ocean up; I become a teapot; I become Francine; dying becomes sport.

* * *

I was young and strong and believed in goodness but when sometimes I saw old horrible things happening I was afraid to interfere.

The Moon Is Over Alstead

One

Your problem's good to work out summer to summer. The hot
air has been tamed, backroads taken back. You want floor space
to unwrinkle the creases of thought. You're not to be fooled. The
second story of a first house is told, that what this pond is, is it,
what it is along with changes. The cherry tree side facing the gold
fields looks dark as the middle of night and gradually over the
day's passing reverses. Calm enough to love with breezy hearts, the
pregnant cows come down. Very few days are perfect. I slept like
a hard dreaming rock. Where the crickets have begun, coffee and
aspirin must begin to work on the project of the day as a pop-up
book. I find the cow's afterbirth in the driveway where the dog's
dragged it to let me know there's a calf. The mind's run off; most all
of us had ancestors who left their homelands once.

Two

One cow joins another in the shade for a cigarette, or is it a heat
wave? My brain is the huff puff engine. My body is a sedan. Water
invites reflections. It's the air's decision. His head is clean and he
drinks an iced drink at the pond. The people in town want to touch
him with their rakes and canes. Follow the hoofprints backwards to
the beginning. Brown cow paused from her licking and mooing to
see the field she'd forgotten. She will have to live with that. Time is
a woman; you've got *that* right. You might get to meaning but it's
deeply squishy.

I'm sorry this is not my permanent life and the pond never gives
birth. One air moves out. They said strong winds. They said once
and for all. Who among us dares to plunge into the colder and
murky depths of longer time? Brown mama cow butts black mama's
baby hard. A junk refrigerator floats in the quarry and the body
in it is my old one. The pull is gravity, down. The float is up, and
the game. Look how easy it is to walk into the radio! If I've just
had coffee and good loving, my feelings on death are bound to be
upbeat. About the moon and the magazines, let the famous smoke
themselves. I'm not sure we *need* ten toes. The mind sets up a studio
and wails. The animal kingdom is angry.

Three

Plant life hangs on. You and I have to look around as things change slowly and quickly. We have a secret in my heart now. The orange mushroom jacket growing on dead logs surprises. Without variety, space is space. We'll be moths and capture all forlorn. No one in your building will give you love or money but I will ask them for these for you and more.

Four

Let's look at sounds: voices in the forest turned to geese. Christine
in her little boat, when the river was flat and the foliage reflected
yellow, was quiet, but quiet like it's nothing. Light in the cobwebbed
screen showed a thousand abstract marks we are dying to believe. If
only you'd known me then! Then we're clean and lighter from the
new snow with sun on it and colored leaves all over it. We have soft
family lungs. Watch very carefully the changes.

The moon's full and I said to Jo I'd like to be on it. We'd be gone
like weed seeds sitting on the high tension tower, dead for the
same infinity that is our space to fall through. Who is there but the
pronouns? They have vulnerable dopamine systems. When the
phone rings, people want money. The pond is one of two small
collection bowls. The work becomes public. The pond's an early
slush freeze kept open by all that plops slush in. Everything wants
to be sucked into the earth. I hear it all falling down. The artist's
husband is an artist too. His wet clothes sprinkled my pillow when
he kissed me. The little boy fell off the bed and hit his head and
had a fit. I am also looking for something else. Flying Boy meets
damaged pear. The stove door's open for the roar and more of the
Cold Lands. One boot lies to the other or it lies alone.

Five

To be all friendly and blab and be nice, I take some artificial light.
The weather boys have trained themselves to be modern. Back on
the good road, their poor little hoofs don't belong on the pavement.
The mist over everything is yellow. All the persons of the people
I love form a blanket of dumbness over me. The dead children
I'm named for drag on me. At the sunflower competition, you had
a terrible headache and napped in the shade tent. The dewdrops
glistened and they were no dreamdrops. The dog burrows her nose
into the snow like she is doing self-reflection.

We know very little about brains. We make up a few pink petals on
a liquor glass wasting away. You ink it up. Boing and you're talking.
Boing again. It's like you got on a plane and went somewhere. Did
you ski both the east loop and the west? Then you're me. You can't
grow grass right up and around a tree trunk. It's a monkey devil
how these trees look. When years later, the boy . . . was troubled,
Billy is tied up and one-by-one the others arrive for bacon. What
Jackie said Mac said. Coffee is my Popeye. The checkbook doesn't
know there's nothing in it. I open the medicine cabinet and there are
three little chickens, one on each shelf.

Six

And then I went away, I go away, I will go away, can slip away. We are happy but we go away, and lie down on the bank on the brink in the heat, and see you, little lizard head in the bush, and see you, Mr. Singapore Red Sealing Wax Palm. Dear Sun, Monday and Tuesday I was in your town, sleeping in the mangles, a magic people pay big money for. It smells like cigarettes and salt water. Should we have stayed home where the lack was no celestial vaulting, as in a released form? Tell me about the medicine garden and the chicks chirping and the bunny spitting up, the hot white high. Everyone else knows nothing. Goodbye to our housekeeping friends.

Seven

The pond's a white field depression in the landscape deep in
our chests, but massive cold climates strengthen the endurance
muscles to achieve excellent hazardous living such as by the great
philosophers of America. We return from dancing at the xylophone
bar. The plankway rolls away. We'll be a couple in New Hampshire
in a gray living room January sunset, a baby yawn learning to
use the potty. We'll drink peculiar beer-sucking emptiness. The
cold finds the hole, rushes in, and freezes the pipe. I listen to him
breathing over the phone. A Japanese doll holds buckets of degrees,
so she could dump some warmth, but she doesn't. The anti-
possibility men march. They've come to say something, but say
nothing. No precipitation falls. There's nothing like a family with a
new baby, nothing like a baby. How about rats and monkeys?

We become competent and we become extinct. I'm speaking for
dinosaurs and depressives. From the top of my glasses shoots a
dagger to the future. I forget that I am driving and I close my eyes.
I forget I am living. I wake up from a night of not sleeping, find
the word "heart" in your heart, take a pill and go. More than more
Arctic air, what other air comes here ever besides the pond frozen
forever? Say "brazen." Say "stupid." Say, "it's what's happening."
They said she was unusual and serious doing hard dark coffee shop
studies, but I heard her laugh at that. I'm doing nothing to stop this
war. I don't know what to do about war. The dog shit will fall into
the water when the snow and ice thaw.

Eight

Dear Snow, when you thaw, I love to be ridiculous on earth, let go of looking and see, to see for the rest of the day, a distant view of the Connecticut, just a little watercolor and a dream. I try to look away to give the thought some privacy, but she is surrounded by other thoughts from the Cave of Thoughts where they breed and birth and squirm until mature and venturing out to a brain or an electric fence or a hexagram. There's something bad I'm forgetting to think about. If the mountain is bald, the earth is an infant. I come out not knowing where I am and everything knocking on the brain door illegal. If it means washing museum floors forever, I'll imagine what would be out the window if you had a window. Sitting snow sits, underfoot a force.

In the grocery, a man with a long red beard and a garden show, and at the barn sale, two men carrying an iron crib and talking with jerk and snap. It's all better than money. To be honest, it's only my hearing it and then being happy. It was no acid trip (suggesting it was). Then I saw the pond had some green to it. Meanwhile I watched the bombing on TV. Water looked like water. It's too late for this American sunlight and too soon to be thinking this way, but thinking likes to get a jump on things.

The outlet waters rush over Three Board Bridge. This is the journey you do staying still, the hard part knowing if you're moving at all. The water molecules rise with no comment. Light hail and the corpse of a small animal get pushed downstream. The disposition to be good is sad at dusk again. The sun has sighed. The moon is over Alstead. To be sincere as water, I need more time alone than I've planned for the radio from Rob's van parked at Jay's barn reminds me. I have to take care of little spring. It is a bowl full of water needing holding. It's in the sap pans smoking and old house wood on fire. I want to be the hand on your forehead that you ask for.

Nine

Oh, what a party was last night! I'm awake now and acquiescing to a complicated argument. I'm happy for him laughing at the TV, cake, movie, party, rain, but I don't want what most people want. A pair of ducks races by on the current of Oh My Little Ashuelot when I stand on the bridge and bow both ways to the river. The abigail, the jehu, and the ostler, I feel lonely when I drive away from them. I meet Tiffany and Eli in the woods on an egg hunt. Their eggs are full of money. Many outside chores need doing and without bugs, it would be time to do them, but instead I lie down and some green emerges where the body warms the ground that freezes it. Mark throws his brain into the river and feels better. Fanny plays the violin seven ways and yells at us to eat more. Jayne reads her thirty-two poems. I am thinking about my debate with Greg. I am firm as a rock, will not flatter or neglect.

All this comes together on a cold wild lake under the mountains with trees just budding up red. Drifting, but not towards sleep, I hear peepers driving home. They drive fast. Too much is good at once. In the center of the round table covered with a cloth held down by five stones is a huge bowl of doubts. Mine are the smallest of problems. Your whole purpose might die with you. What do I give you? What do I take? A bit about that: your hand wants a kiss. Now we're two steps removed. I can't reach your hand to my lips. Trees go up and down. Sky is up and down. If it's beautiful once, it's more beautiful twice. When I eat bread and butter I'm happy while I'm eating it. No one can see me. I have flowers in my face. It's not a bad thing, flowers in the face. It's serious which means it's funny and it changes clothes in my mind. My naked thought's clothes lie in messy heaps.

66

Mann says that Goethe says that beauty is shame-faced because she rouses desire which conflicts with the spiritual she represents. Not for me. Tonight the frogs will sing their love songs under a lunar eclipse. The dandelion thinks he's God and I think he loves me, but love needs no object. Our eyes are somewhere further out in the plain. They're soloing. We're soloing. Have we done enough? Is there no end? Meanwhile, we'll do what we said we would.

Ten

We come all the way to Bull Creek to learn to go the way we go. Knee deep we know we can do it and do it quickly, dive down to the original problem. We watch our hands come together and push apart in the murk. The water certainly is getting warmer.

Hover, hover dragonfly who doesn't need to know me or this or the color blue which he is. How about hats? We're not afraid of heights. And the fence between us has jumpable gaps.

RECENT TITLES FROM ALICE JAMES BOOKS

Here, Bullet, Brian Turner
The Far Mosque, Kazim Ali
Gloryland, Anne Marie Macari
Polar, Dobby Gibson
Pennyweight Windows: New & Selected Poems, Donald Revell
Matadora, Sarah Gambito
In the Ghost-House Acquainted, Kevin Goodan
The Devotion Field, Claudia Keelan
Into Perfect Spheres Such Holes Are Pierced, Catherine Barnett
Goest, Cole Swensen
Night of a Thousand Blossoms, Frank X. Gaspar
Mister Goodbye Easter Island, Jon Woodward
The Devil's Garden, Adrian Matejka
The Wind, Master Cherry, the Wind, Larissa Szporluk
North True South Bright, Dan Beachy-Quick
My Mojave, Donald Revell
Granted, Mary Szybist
Sails the Wind Left Behind, Alessandra Lynch
Sea Gate, Jocelyn Emerson
An Ordinary Day, Xue Di
The Captain Lands in Paradise, Sarah Manguso
Ladder Music, Ellen Doré Watson
Self and Simulacra, Liz Waldner
Live Feed, Tom Thompson
The Chime, Cort Day
Utopic, Claudia Keelan
Pity the Bathtub Its Forced Embrace of the Human Form,
    Matthea Harvey
Isthmus, Alice Jones
The Arrival of the Future, B.H. Fairchild
The Kingdom of the Subjunctive, Suzanne Wise
Camera Lyrica, Amy Newman
How I Got Lost So Close to Home, Amy Dryansky
Zero Gravity, Eric Gamalinda
The Art of the Lathe, B.H. Fairchild

Alice James Books has been publishing exclusively poetry since 1973. One of the few presses in the country that is run collectively, the cooperative selects manuscripts for publication through both regional and national annual competitions. New regional authors become active members of the cooperative, participating in the editorial decisions of the press. The press, which historically has placed an emphasis on publishing women poets, was named for Alice James, sister of William and Henry, whose fine journal and gift for writing went unrecognized within her lifetime.

Typeset and Designed by Mike Burton

Printed by Thomson-Shore